secret compartment!

A Cherry Street Publication

First published in the United States of America by

Secret Compartment, LLC

Copyright © Secret Compartment, 2020. All rights reserved.

Cover Art and Layout by J. Stiele

Printed and Bound by Lulu.

Copyright © 2002-2020 Lulu Press, Inc. All Rights Reserved.

International Standard Book Number(s) granted in a printing agreement with Lulu Press, Inc.

Library of Congress Cataloguing-in-Publication Data

Cut to the Media. / Scholastica Media Theory and Research

Book - Pages 1 - end – (Humanities)

Includes bibliographical references.

ISBN 978-1-71695-821-2

(printed on acid-free paper)
1. Communication in learning and scholarship-Publication strategies. 2. Scholarly publishing.
3. Humanities-Creative Writing. 4. Humanities-Research.
5. Humanities-Writing for mass media.

2020 2019   2018   2017 4 3 2 1

Cherry Street Publishing

An imprint of Secret Compartment, LLC

1200 Kenwood Avenue

Tower Room 4407 -- Science Studio 1132

Duluth, MN 55811

(dis) CONTENTS

The media; it is a vast concept that we see and hear about every single day in the United States, whether it's referring to mainstream media sources, like Fox News, CNN, and MSNBC, or social media platforms, such as Twitter, Facebook, Instagram, and the many, many others. While all of these are, for the most part, very different from one another, they have two key things in common:

1– They are all consumed by millions of people across the world, all day, everyday. And,

2– They are all consumed through some sort of smart electronic device.

These devices are mostly, but not limited to, smartphones of any kind, tablets, laptops, desktops, radios, TV's, at-home listening devices such as the Google Nest Hub or Amazon Echo, and yes, even most wrist watches these days. With all of these different devices and technologies around us, we have grown quite used to them being a part of our daily lives. But what most people don't know is that the technologies within these devices could be the precursor to living in a nation where you are constantly being watched and listened to.

After reading that sentence, you might be thinking, "oh god, not another conspiracy theory!" But please, let me assure you, this is no conspiracy; it's actually a reality in multiple countries around the world. Let me explain… two rather well-known countries located in Eastern Asia have been living in what is known as a "surveillance state" for the past several years. A surveillance state is more or less when a nation's government takes part in the mass surveillance of its people, usually to obtain information and keep a close eye on its citizens and outsiders[1].

---

[1] "Defining the Surveillance State." Privacy International. Accessed April 15, 2020.

I'll start with one of the more extreme examples of surveillance states. North Korea, the first of the two Eastern Asian countries that I mentioned above, is not only a surveillance state but a Socialist State as well. North Koreans have been under strict watch by their leader, Kim Jong-Un, for many years now, mostly to keep track of its citizens. According to Andrei Nikolaevich Lankov, In-ok Kwak, and Choong-Bin Cho's Article, *The Organizational Life: Daily Surveillance and Daily Resistance in North Korea,* North Korean citizens are required to attend events called "Organizational Life" up to 3 times a week. These are used to keep track of citizens using a "highly formalized array of surveillance and indoctrination practices that are conducted within a set of networks, each run by a particular government-controlled organization[2].

For surveillance, other than thousands of cameras, the North Korean Government relies on its own citizens to keep track of each other. Again, according to Lankov, Kwak, and Cho, the citizens are required to engage in "an exercise of self-policing," where they watch one another and report any suspicious activity or wrongdoing to a formal authority like the police[3]. This act of citizens basically criticising their neighbors keeps crime rates low and the people under control. Unless a serious accusation is made, most people will report anything they see to an officer at an Organizational Life meeting.

Another part of this meeting is the "indoctrination practices," which I mentioned above. It is another form of surveillance used by the North Korean Government. These required practices are given to preselected citizens who give reports of government happenings. During these reports, a lot of propaganda and messages of praise to President Jong-Un and his administration are given, and it is at this time, that citizens turn in their reports of what they've seen their neighbors do, if anything. These weekly organizations of the North Korean community easily allows its government to keep a close eye over their people.

---

[2] Lankov, Kwak, and Cho. "The Organizational Life: Daily Surveillance and Daily Resistance in North Korea." *Journal of East Asian Studies* 12
[3] Ibid.

The second Eastern Asian country is China. China's approach is a lot different than North Korea's. You see, China relies heavily on their technology rather than their control to keep track of all 1.4 billion of its people. According to Xiao Qiang's article, *The Road to Digital Unfreedom: President Xi's Surveillance State,* in 2012, China's government started requiring its citizens to use their real names when using the internet. This means they have to use their legal names that the government has on any sort of virtual account they make for themselves online. Qiang continues to say that in 2013, the Chinese Government passed a law that "authorized prison terms of up to three years for the posting of comments that spread rumors and are deemed to be defamatory.[4] This means that the government can and will be watching the Chinese citizens' internet posts and searches to keep track of what they're doing.

Other than internet data tracking, China also has the world's largest system of public cameras, which by now in 2020, have voice and facial recognition technologies. These cameras are constantly watching, whether it's on the busy streets or inside apartment buildings, and they can spot a possible "event of interest," in Qiang's words, and tag that event as a possible threat and contact the appropriate authority. According to a report given by China Central Television, SenseNet, a major tech company in China, completed their "Skynet" project in 2017. The Skynet project is the world's largest video-surveillance system that included 176 million surveillance cameras at that time. Many of these cameras are AI-equipped, which means that they can monitor the clothing, gender, height, and possible age of any given passer byer[5]. Now in 2020, according to Qiang, the system has grown astronomically, nearing around 626 million cameras.

---

[4] Qiang, Xiao. "The Road to Digital Unfreedom: President Xi's Surveillance State."
Journal of Democracy 30
[5] Ibid.

Eric Mistry is a Instructional Technologist & Digital Media Specialist with a Master's in Business Administration at The College of St. Scholastica in Duluth, Minnesota. I was fortunate enough to get an interview with him and hear his opinions as a person with expertise in this field. When asked "what kind of effect do these technologies have on a country like China," Mistry said, "It's a double-edged sword to be honest. On a positive note, these could be incredibly useful technologies for saving lives, preventing crime, and optimizing cities to be as ideal as possible. On a more realistic note, these technologies are a totalitarian government's dream. They allow total control and surveillance, even prediction. The power added by AI means that a small number of individuals can actually comb through massive amounts of data. In simpler terms, this means that the power of the government to surveil and control its population is massively increased and able to be controlled by a select few".[6]

Now, you're probably thinking what I first thought when I learned this information. "Sure, I could see this happening in countries like these, but never here in the US… at least not to this extent." But what most people don't know, or don't think about, is that the US is just as technologically advanced as China, if not more so, and produces incredible amounts of data that can be tracked. From streaming *Tiger King* on Netflix to posting a meme on Instagram to texting your girlfriend or boyfriend on your iPhone 11, we are constantly using trackable and mappable data.

The most recent example of using our own data to track us comes out of the shadow casted by COVID-19, or the Novel CoronaVirus. As it has swept across the US, most state governors passed "Stay-at-home" orders, which meant people shouldn't go outside, except for essential things such as getting groceries or exercise. But, with Americans being Americans, we couldn't stay cooped up in our homes for very long. We started going outside, going to beaches, and hanging out with our friends– against the orders of our elected officials. To combat this and

---

[6] Mistry, Eric. Interview by Jacob Stiele. Personal Interview, March 30, 2020.

keep track of who was where, some well-known, major tech companies, such as Google and Apple, began to track the movements of their users.

According to Casey Newton, a journalist for *The Verge,* an American technology news website, "Google is using location data gathered from smartphones to help public health officials understand how people's movements have changed in response to the global COVID-19 pandemic."[7] Google and public health officials then use the collected data for statistics such as a rough estimate of who is listening to the stay-at-home orders, amount of people going to super markets, going to work/ offices, going to parks, etc. etc.

The silver lining in this is that, so far, only people who have given consent to Google and Apple have had their locations shared. That means when your phone, laptop, watch, or whatever-device asks you, "May we use your current location?" and you click, "Yes," you could possibly be adding yourself to the statistics listed above.

Continuing in my interview with Mistry, he commented on the idea of these technologies becoming more prominent in the US. "With proper open audits, third-party watch dogs, and transparent code, this technology could save lives, prevent crime and other trouble, and make society more efficient. A good example (and now a real one) is a grocery store that can recognize who you are and what you pick out, so you can get groceries without ever needing to go through the checkout line. (Amazon is already doing this with their Go Stores) The AI might even recognize that you forgot an item on your list and notify you before you leave. The trickier thing is where the line is drawn and who gets access to information, both private and "public", for the purpose of feeding it to the AI."[8]

----

[7] Newton, Casey. "Google Uses Location Data to Show Which Places Are Complying with Stay-at-Home Orders - and Which Aren't." The Verge. The Verge, April 3, 2020.
[8] Mistry, Personal Interview.

So I'm going to leave it up in the air for you to decide. I could see arguments made for both sides, but ultimately, as a benefit of being a US citizen, we get certain unalienable rights and freedoms; rights to our privacy and freedom to speak what we want. While this is a growing reality here, I do not think it will become as much of a surveillance state as China. HOWEVER, I do believe that what we currently have, such as tech companies tracking our movements, facial recognition in street cameras, and AI's that know what you need when you go to the grocery store, will continue to grow and spread within the US as times progresses uncertainty towards the future.

2. Memes: Alternative Purposes and Detrimental Consequences
Emily Manning

Memes are increasingly evident in our online societies. They appear in many different forms, and can be described in a multitude of ways. People often come across memes in their daily lives, whether intentionally looking for them, or not. A research study conducted in 2019 showed that 38% of people specifically follow meme accounts on social media.[9] Memes have the tendency to pollute our media sites, several of them quickly arriving across various social media platforms. Today, memes are even becoming a popular, and interestingly effective, method of online marketing. While I have always been an eager consumer of memes, it was only recently I became aware of their alternative purposes. By examining collected research from digital culture on social media platforms, I expect my studies to reveal that memes have negative societal implications through the process of desensitization, the spread of misinformation, and through elements of group conformity.

The word 'meme' was first produced from a book titled *The Selfish Gene*, authored by Richard Dawkins. From Dawkins perspective, memes were first thought of as "mannerisms, skills, or other behavioral/informational

---

[9] YPulse, "3 Stats That Show What Memes Mean to Gen Z & Millennials." April 22, 2020.

components that were either taught directly or transmitted by imitation - any non-genetic behavior qualified as a meme".[10] Customarily, memes can now be depicted as "a piece of culture, typically a joke, which gains influence through online transmission".[11] Generally, ordinary forms of memes are presented as images, frequently taken out of context, and accompanied by a clever text caption. This formatting is referred to as an image macro. Image macros are visual aids combined with worded captions to present a preconstructed ideal, making them strikingly similar to memes that appear in our well known digital societies.

I conducted an interview with an owner of a meme account that has around forty-thousand followers, called @minnesotamemes. My interviewee, Ben Nesvig, not only manages his personal meme account, but also creates memes for digital marketing purposes. Companies like *Chex Mix, Bugles, General Mills, Kwik Trip, Gushers,* and *Netflix* all have their own meme accounts that he, and members of his team, design memes for as camouflaged advertisements. He is employed by a company called *The Social Lights,* where the entrance to their building of operations displays a culturally significant meme mural featuring Kermit the frog sipping *Lipton* tea, Doge, a dancing Drake, a weeping Michael Jordan, and other acknowledged memes.

During our interview, we discussed the effortless reciprocation of memes. This is increasingly prevalent, and is apparent in our current society - especially regarding the current pandemic, and *Netflix's* recent docuseries release of *Tiger King.* Noticing what's getting emotional reactions from people at the moment, and basing memes off of concepts or events widely recognized in the current state of the media seems to be a popular trend in the production of memes. We also conversed about how memes are difficult to define, but easy to identify. Nesvig views memes as "a vehicle of communicating an idea or information in a way that's super efficient, and usually highly

---

[10] Scott & Bill. "Memes: The Interaction Between Imagery and Subculture: An Analysis of Situation, Race, and Gender on the Pi Kappa Delta Social Media App". *Forensic* 103.
[11] Ibid.

shareable".[12] It's beneficial for readers to recognize that this definition comes from a marketing point of view. We both admitted to sharing memes via direct messaging or explicitly tagging another party in a post at least once a day, emphasizing the accessible shareability aspect of memes in our personal lives. However, sharing appears to be a fundamental facet of social media as a whole, as research suggests 55% of 13-35 year-olds send memes every week, while 30% of these users share memes everyday.

Regarding the uncomplicated act of distributing and sharing memes, I'd like to examine how they contribute to the spread of misinformation. Wardle, an author with a knowledgeable background in the spread of

misinformation, said "Humans are wired to respond to emotional triggers and share misinformation if it reinforces existing beliefs and

---

[12] Nesvig, Ben. Interview by Emily Manning. Personal Interview, April 10, 2020.

prejudices," and so many memes are constructed to do just that.[13] The weaponization of misinformation via memes was rampant and

extensive, particularly on *Facebook* during the 2016 presidential election. Russian affiliates contrived meme content containing extremely controversial issues and positioned them in voter's timelines to reinforce and accentuate pre-existing biases, among other outcomes they had intended to cause panic and escalate confusion through these satire communication methods.

I believe memes contribute to the desensitization of their audience by frequently promoting repulsive and outdated gender roles, the constant objectification of women, dehumanization, racism, sexism, violence, xenophobic traits, etc. In most cases, desensitization can be defined as "the reduction or eradication of cognitive, emotional, physiological, and ultimately behavioral responses to a stimulus".[14] In a chapter of *The Oxford Handbook of Media Psychology* authored by psychology professor Jeanne Brockmyer, she explains that desensitization is a

---

[13] Wardle, Claire. "A New World Disorder." *Scientific American 321. No 3: 88.*

[14] Brockmyer, Jeanne F. "Media Violence, Desensitization, and Psychological Engagement." *Oxford University Press.* 212-20.

normal and adaptive response to unpleasant emotional events. As humans, we are not capable of prolonged authentic emotional responses to other people's catastrophes. While many initially feel compelled to lend a hand to others during trying times, our desire to extend our help inevitably begins to deplete when ourselves are not being directly affected.

How does this relate to memes? Well, the theory of mere exposure, first proposed by social psychologist Robert Zajonc, suggests that upon an individual's repeated exposure to a particular stimulus item, their attitude toward that item will gradually have an altered or less emotional response.[15] When people are continuously bombarded and exposed to memes that emphasize stereotypes, sexism, anarchism, and other "-isms", it leads these individuals to participate in displaying implicit biases. Thus, negatively changing their behaviors in social interactions. When this interpretation is applied to a mass populous, readers can begin to conceptualize how this would alter our societal norms.   Ultimately, this notion invites me to ponder what content the upcoming generations will perceive as socially acceptable.

Sharing is highly valued on social media, and a prominent feature of memes, especially when accompanied by the concept of deindividuation. Historically, it has been known that humans behave differently in groups than when they are alone. Deindividuation aims attention toward these alternative behaviors, looking at how being in groups "causes people to become less aware of themselves and less concerned with how others will evaluate them. Because being in a large group makes a person more aroused and more anonymous, the person focuses less on themselves and behaves more impulsively".[16] Consider this approach in a social media environment, where anonymity is enhanced, and that the large group in this context refers to millions of users around the globe. What kind of future are we manifesting for our

---

[15] Gass & Seiter. "Persuasion: Social Influence and Compliance Gaining." *S.I.:CRC Press.* 199.
[16] Ibid, 135.

civilization, and will these elements of our digital society someday become merged with our genuine existence?

Another concept we can begin to look at is the group polarization phenomenon. This phenomenon suggests that "groups cause people to become more extreme in their decisions. Thus, if you are predisposed to making a slightly risky decision, being in a group may cause you to make a riskier decision".[17] The United States nation saw an example of this when the "Storm Area 51, They Can't Stop All of Us" campaign was trending, and some of the drastic measures people took to fulfill this objective. Thinking about this and the deindividuation concept together, we begin to see an online society in which actions or things said won't have as severe, or as many, consequences as they do in reality. Then we must consider how this will persist in affecting civilization. These memes are liked, usually commented on in a vulgar manner, and they are shared at an alarmingly rapid scale and rate. The punchline of a meme may be something an individual would personally *never* make fun of, but still may find the meme funny when another person has already put it out there. It's become normalized, and it absolutely contributes to desensitization among their other repercussions - like by enhancing the effects of the social comparison theory.

---

17 Ibid, 141.

The social comparison theory, in short, suggests that individuals determine things about themselves by making comparisons to other people. Let's dig into a deeper examination of this theory and find out what makes it relative to group conformity. Persuasion textbook authors, Robert Gass and John Seiter, determined that according to this theory, many people prefer to view, and compare, themselves in a positive manner. These individuals often fear mediocrity, aspiring to be more than just average. "According to this theory, when people learn that their position is the same as that of everyone else in the group, they shift their position so that it is more extreme. Because everyone tends to do this, group polarization occurs".[18]

Regarding memes, I often see many of them containing content that is relatable, making comparison for audiences easy. With this comparison comes the insistence of the extreme positions viewers frequently begin to verbalize in comment sections - and this especially occurs for memes that display political aims or biases. There are collections of humans that crave and relish attention, many of them appearing in these comment sections and producing their own content with the intention of gaining popularity. Memes are often composed with no motives alternative to gaining mass attraction across digital platforms, allowing for content to be anything that will grab one's attention. Using the 2016 presidential election as an example once more, it is evident that the results of this type of sharing have critical aftereffects on people's lives.

Taking the abundant negative outcomes from memes into consideration, the spread of misinformation, the process of desensitization, and elements of group conformity are discernible. Memes have great potential to be vessels of misinformation, they contribute to dulling our emotional reactions to images that *should* provoke emotional responses, and elements of group conformity enhances their potential effects in digital society. I still thoroughly enjoy certain memes, and am still a reluctant participant in sharing them. However, with their alternative purposes and deceptive motives in

---

[18] Ibid, 142.

mind, I now critically monitor and analyze the content that appears in memes to avoid strengthening these preferred outcomes. To conclude, as a student of media studies, I firmly believe it is crucial for communities to be aware of this concept.

As technology advances and ingrains itself into society, so does the challenge of detecting false information. The rising use of social media in recent years has resulted in users having to sift through information to determine what is true and what is false. A Pew Research Center study conducted just after the 2016 election found 64% of adults believe fake news stories cause a great deal of confusion and 23% said they had shared fabricated political stories themselves – sometimes by mistake and sometimes intentionally.[19] Misinformation contaminating social media platforms may be attributed to bias or a lack of discernment and critical thinking among the general public.

Misinformation entails much more than "fake news" and stems from many locations— some even from within ourselves. The growth of fake news is very easy in the current era where most people get their 'news' via social media[20] If social media is becoming a leading news source, citizens must be sure that the news being produced on social media is accurate and of high quality. To relieve social media of the plague that is misinformation, one must first go back to its origins to find out why and how it permeates these platforms.

One of the ways that misinformation can pervade social media platforms is through our own biases. A 2018 study administered by Pew Research Center indicated that Americans tend to label statements they agree with as factual and those they disagree with as opinion.[21] When personal biases play a role in what enters your social media news feed, it isn't always deliberate. This could happen after you go on Facebook and see one of your Facebook friends put up a post that you don't

---

[19] Anderson and Raine, The Future of Truth and Misinformation Online." Pew Research Center: Internet, Science & Tech. Pew Research Center, December 31, 2019.
[20] Ibid.
[21] Eberhart, Media Literacy, 2018.

particularly like or agree with. If you see this post and unfriend them, you are already filtering your social media site to align with only your beliefs and others who are like-minded.

Additionally, misinformation may make its way to our newsfeeds simply through our own lack of understanding. Cultural barriers display this when a "meme" or an image macro, or some other form of information is shared globally. The information may be translated from one culture and language to another. Within this translation, there is always the possibility that the meaning of the message may not translate precisely.

Another way that misinformation can become a part of the media is simply by an exaggerated headline. Carys Jeffrey, social and digital marketer spoke on the issue of exaggerated headlines from the media's point of view saying, "A big reason I've found that many sites have these exaggerated headlines is in order to drive traffic to their site and also get clicks on the ads on their site or donations to their organization. It's all money for them. More shares – more clicks – more income. They put that above ethics."[22] She also touched on the peril of these headlines when she stated, "the weight of sharing misinformation is definitely overlooked now. Many people tend to share an article based on it's headline – possibly without even fully reading the article – or look for headlines that fulfil their opinion. They don't realise that spreading misinformation can cause something as drastic as changing the course of an election."[23] These are only a few instances of many where misinformation may infiltrate social media.

Many professionals in the field are not entirely optimistic that the situation will improve in the coming years. The term "fake news" became particularly popular after the 2016 presidential election and has stayed so ever since. Emmanuel Edet, head of legal services at the National Information Technology Development Agency of Nigeria, observed, "The information environment will improve but at a cost to

---

[22] Jeffrey, Carys. Personal Interview, 2020.
[23] Ibid.

privacy."[24] Edet suggests that an effective method to improve the expansion of misinformation in the media is to closely monitor what is being put onto the internet. However, the line between freedom of speech and filtering out false information is not so black and white.

Another professional in the field, Julia Koller, a learning solutions lead developer, stated "Information is only as reliable as the people who are receiving it. If readers do not change or improve their ability to seek out and identify reliable information sources, the information environment will not improve."[25] Koller insinuates that the spread of misinformation is a human problem, not a technology one. She advises that humans must take action and do their own critical thinking if there is to be any improvement.

Another origin of misinformation could derive from something as simple as a deficiency of critical thinking. In fact, a recent and very relevant study on the spread of misinformation regarding COVID-19 in the media has corroborated such, stating, "We find support for the idea that people share false claims about COVID-19 in part because they simply neglect to think sufficiently about whether or not content is accurate when deciding what to share."[26]

Lastly, in concurrence with Koller, Christian H. Huitema, former president of the Internet Architecture Board, commented "The quality of information will not improve in the coming years, because technology can't improve human nature all that much."[27] It is human nature to share these posts that we see that are outrageous, even if they are clearly false. Although, it generally backfires as the post only obtains more popularity and traction from every share, both positive and negative. While simply not sharing is the best approach, Jeffrey offers a solution

---

[24] Anderson and Raine, The Future, 2019.

[25] Ibid.

[26] Pennycook and Rand, Fighting COVID-19, 2019.

[27] Anderson and Raine.

to sharing this false information for the purpose of showing that it is false. In an interview, she revealed

> "One thing I've seen a huge push for on Twitter is if you disagree with someone – don't 'quote tweet' them to say it, but screenshot their original tweet and then add your copy to the tweeted screenshot image. I think that has the same value as a shared incorrect article – don't share the article source because that only looks good for the source and encourages clicks and income for them. Share a screenshot or write your own post quoting them but refrain from sharing the original article."[28]

Returning to and considering the recently mentioned COVID-19 pandemic, the spread of misinformation has never been more pertinent. COVID-19 has brought online rumors of natural cures, alleged origins of the virus, and even natural testing methods for COVID-19. One example has been a widespread, alleged natural testing method to hold your breath for ten seconds. If this action is practicable for you, according to many Twitter user's, then you are negative for COVID-19. This statement acquired a lot of traction, making it seem more credible and therefore resulting in many people believing this claim. When researching the origins of these claims though, one will only discover accounts with no sources to justify their claims. The present pandemic is not the first instance of distrust that the public has encountered with the scientific community. In fact, this disconnect has been an ongoing battle. One of the more modern and sizable conflicts between the scientific community and the general public has revolved around vaccines. This divide has seemed to split the public into two groups: those who support scientific claims and anti-vaxxers.

The key takeaway of both circumstances of divisions between science and the public has remained the same: "Spread of false information drowns out credible sources and in turn results in further public

---

[28] Jeffrey, Carys. Personal Interview, 2020

confusion, ultimately leading to greater spread, and inefficient mitigation of virus transmission."[29] If government leaders and media would remain consistent for the public during these times and use sources providing accurate information, such as the CDC, it would be easier to "...manage, educate, and address the people's concerns, there is an opportunity to bridge the level of distrust that has arisen by anti science movements in recent times."[30] It is not an uncomplicated mission to maintain that all news is unvarying and fact-based.

There is a lot of pressure put onto large companies to do this and filter through the false information such as the vaccination claims to change the current circumstances. "Several fact-checking initiatives have been started...some rely on human raters, while others rely on automated tools."[31] Numerous platforms already have algorithms in place to help filter through the information put onto their sites, but people don't seem to think that the current system is doing enough. It may be due to the fact that "most platforms still hold the position 'if it's not criminal, it's free speech'... they take the money, and leave the costly work (fact-checking, counter-arguing, etc.) to journalists from media outlets."[32] Jeffrey also says that with these platforms being privatised companies they're not really required to do anything at all or bound by any governing body to be told what to do."[33]

News editor and manager of an online newspaper at Minnesota State University Moorhead, Ashley Johnson, agrees that free speech is the main reason that social media platform executives don't do more to intercept misinformation in the media.[34] Johnson's message for the public is that "If you haven't heard of the source, it is wise to look further before deciding to trust the information."[35] Johnson also says that "if

---

[29] Mian and Khan, Coronavirus, 2020.
[30] Ibid.
[31] Moravec et al., eds., Fake News, 2018.
[32] Newman, Journalism, 2020.
[33] Jeffrey, Personal Interview, 2020.
[34] Johnson, Personal Interview, 2020
[35] Ibid

one shares the information stating it is false, they are a part of the problem. Anything that brings more traffic to these sites gives them more incentive to post and create more of it".[36] Resist the urge to share, even if it is to discredit the post.

It all seems to culminate to a human problem as many of the professionals in the industry have concurred. People make their own choices to access and take in information via the particular method of social media. Jeffrey adds to this saying "It's human nature to want to be correct – spreading information that you agree with (whether it's factually accurate or otherwise) is a great way to get that satisfaction…humans want the validation that comes with their opinion or viewpoint being seen as 'factual news'. The people behind the screen writing these [exaggerated] headlines and deliberately putting out the fake news are led by money and not ethos. The privatised social media companies have more to gain by their platform being used – even if it's people sharing misinformation it still equates to money for them as well."[37]

Ultimately, whether or not the media is willing to step up and stand for ethos over money or whether or not they are able to enforce filtration of content, the public must first become educated on this issue and respond by becoming researchers of a sort. It is up to the public to improve their news quality by being skeptical, discerning, aware of their own biases, and by using objective analysis of the information in front of them.

[36] Johnson, Personal Interview, 2020
[37] Jeffrey, Personal Interview, 2020

There is so much misinformation out there in the world. One of the big outlets that could be seen as the cause of this is the news outlets. There are so many different outlets out there it can be hard to distinguish what information is true or not. As there are also many hurdles that journalists must go through to make sure their information is accurate. We are seeing to be very true with the events of COVID-19. "Ministers say that they have launched a 'Rapid Response Unit' aimed at stopping false stories before they are circulated(...)the government has already identified seventy incidents this week and are working to take them down."[38]

Now this may seem like an isolated event but there have been cases of misinformation in the news before. An example of this would be Fox News. "Co-anchor Bill Hemmer cited a Texans false claim that the wall built in El Paso caused crime rate to drop by 90%. When the truth was El Paso already reached a historically low crime rate before the Congress authorized a fence in 2006."[39] "Anchor Neil Cavuto claimed that Democrats supported the wall under Obama, implying they changed their position when Trump proposed the wall. When the facts were after a failed comprehensive immagration bill in 2013 Democrats voted to have the Department of Homeland Security examine where fencing would be needed."[40].

But why does misinformation spread so easily? There has been research done on this before in order to see what the process behind this is. " In summer 2017, Davidson College, a private liberal arts college, incoming first-year students completed an hour-long mini-course for the

---

[38] Independent.Co.Uk
[39] Media Matters, The Fox News Lie, 8.
[40] Ibid, 12.

library as part of an orientation requirement. The researchers' aim for the mini-course was to understand how incoming first-year students consume and evaluate news in digital environments."[41] The researchers did a few different exercises to see if these students could evaluate if the news article was real or not. Such as looking at Imposter URLs, which is where hackers create fake websites that look similar to the real deal.

Focusing mainly on exercise three the results where that many students struggled with identifying the imposter url was very difficult. "One finding underscores this issue students reported a willingness to share fake news. Of all the stories students engaged with in the exercises, the story from Exercise 3 (Impostor URL) was the one they indicated they would most readily share. However, most who reported they would share the story were not completely confident in its accuracy.(...) Each set of student responses to the exercises contained notable trends. One trend across all exercises was the tendency for students to mention that they would like to examine additional sources as part of [42]their evaluative process."

So it seems that more people are willing to share stories over social media. While some people may question the imposter url that they see it is clearly shown that the students who did evaluate the fake news article had very little confidence in evaluating whether this was the real website or not. Now given that there are some people out there who most likely cannot evaluate the differences between a real website and a fake one, many people will just share it because it seems like a legitimate news article.

When it comes to writing a news article event there have been situations where news articles contained misinformation, but what are some issues journalists have to deal with when investigating a topic for an article? "What it seems to be is when you are looking for things on

---

[41] How Students Evaluate the News, 4.
[42] Ibid, 11.

Google, the Google algorithm will show you articles that will appeal to what you have searched online, and the consumer will listen to those articles or not."[43] There have also been situations where news outlets will nitpick certain information to fit their narrative. As we saw examples earlier of Fox News claiming something is true when in reality it was either not true or they left out some very important context to the situation. "There have been situations where people will nitpick information because they are looking for clarification on a topic, but it is the journalists job to be as clear as possible." (Baihley Marie, Interview) [44] It can also be very hard for journalists to get unbiased information. "There are different sets of opinions, what the 'real' opinion is can have different opinions and [45]interpretations about the facts." (Dr. Nathan Carroll, Interview). There are ways for reporters to put checks in place, but it doesn't always stop people from being biased. "When a reporter writes something down, it gets reviewed to make sure it is fair, but at the end of the day no one is completely unbiased on certain topics." (Baihley Marie, Interview)[46] There are many issues journalists have to face when trying to get accurate information for a news article, but there is still a level of responsibility journalists do have when writing an article.

News journalists work very hard to give people accurate information on a topic or an event. But aside from that they cannot control the rate that misinformation can travel. " Among fact-checked news, fake articles were more likely than real articles to "go viral" on social media. (...) Regardless of whether one believes a piece of fake news, prior encounters with it can reduce how unethical one thinks spreading it would be." (Misinformation and Morality, pg.76)[47] If we keep seeing these articles, people will think that it would be okay to share, perhaps thinking that if so many people are sharing this article, there must be truth to it. There have been studies done online to see if people see a

---

[43] Dr. Nathan Carroll Interview.

[44] Baihley Marie Interview.

[45] Dr. Nathan Carroll Interview.

[46] Baihley Marie Interview.

[47]Misinformation and Morality, 76.

fake news article more than once, would they share the article then? "Intuitively, previous encounters with fake-news headlines made those headlines seem less unethical to publish, which correlated in a mediation analysis with a stronger inclination to "like" and share those headlines and a weaker inclination to block or unfollow someone who shared them consistent with the results of our prior experiments." (Misinformation and Morality, pg. 82)[48]

There are ways that many people have been trying their hardest to make sure their information is correct. But it is still incredibly hard to stop the spread of misinformation. There is still the small majority that will take that misinformation and present it as facts if it fits their own narrative. Even if there is a news network that an individual trusts, it can be good to have a healthy level of skepticism, and do your own research on a topic.

---

[48]Misinformation and Morality, 82.

5. How much does
The Internet know
about me?
Dan Salutz

I think by this point all of us know that there is information about us on the internet, whether it's our address or some other arbitrary thing, but what about other things? In today's digital age you can find out information about a person with a few clicks, in fact you can find out a lot about yourself even quicker. Did you know that Google tracks not only your search history but your movement, any emails you've sent or received, including junk mail and spam, and finally your travel information. For those who are unaware, Google, when you have your location turned on can track every step you take with your phone in your possession and turned on. In a 2018 article tech consultant Dylan Curren showed through a series of tweets how much information Google has in its possession. In the article Curren shares a series of maps, code, and files that were sent to him by Google when he requested his data from the tech giant. The maps showed every place he had travelled in the last twelve months, the code showed

Through personal experience I've learned just how much information you can find on the internet whether about yourself or friends or family. The first time I really did a search of someone on the internet was when I had a suspicion about a person who a friend of mine was involved in a relationship with and through a simple search of the person's name I found that the person had a pretty extensive criminal record. This information sparked my curiosity and decided to randomly search for people I knew starting with people who were close friends and after some searching found that every court case or hearing that had taken place in my county was available for public view, not only could you see the name of the case but also who was involved and what the charge was. Through this website I found out that a friend of mine had made multiple appearances in court over multiple traffic violations which didn't surprise me necessarily considering I knew how this person drove and had seen them do doughnuts in the school parking lot. The city I reside in also has a blog that shows every person that has been arrested each day over twenty four hours and naturally the text of every single email he sent or received and every event that was every logged in his Google Calendar and finally the files which added up to about five gigabytes of data where every photo, video, and document he had created even the ones he deleted. Curren's experience shows just how scary the internet truly can be and the fact that there is information we didn't even know existed in some cases out there.

This peaked my interest and I after looking through about a weeks worth of arrests found that it was rare that there wasn't a person I at least vaguely recognize, whether it was a person I'd went to highschool with or a person I recognized from just seeing them on the street websites like this have made it a lot

easier to find out information that in the old days you only heard about though gossip.
For the sake of my interest in internet information for my research I conducted a survey of friends and family to see how they felt about the information available on the internet, whether it be about them or people they knew and found their answers were pretty similar. For the survey I asked three questions
1. Have they ever found information about themselves on the internet they didn't know was public

As for my third question one hundred percent of the people I surveyed believed the pros outweigh the cons in regards to information on the internet. One person's rationel was that " in everything there's trade offs and in this case we give up a bit of privacy in exchange for a large amount of convenience". The answers to the questions were probably one I expected but still make me wonder how much information is out there, who knows it and what do they plan to do with it.

2. Were they comfortable with the amount of information about them available on the internet

3. Did they think the positives in knowing this information outweighs the negative. Starting with question one, of the people I surveyed all but one answered yes, common things were voting records, address history and things similar to that. One of the people I surveyed told me they found information on a voting records website that not only was very detailed but was also inaccurate, it had gotten their designated polling place wrong and had said they voted in elections they hadn't. So sometimes the information about you on the internet you didn't know existed isn't even accurate. As for the second question the answers were split fifty fifty, the people that stated that they were comfortable with information stated that there was no information that they would consider harmful so they weren't going to worry about it, one person was quoted saying "well you could easily find out that same information from the phone book so I don't the harm in it being on the internet.

6.   The Walt Disney Company's World Dominance
and Influence on Humanity
Nathaniel Hilton

Over the past few decades, media has become an important part of people's lives, as people seek and obtain information, entertainment, and communication through the media. Media corporations can play a role in audiences' lives; one of those companies is none other than the Walt Disney Company. Most people in western countries will have had contact with Disney ever since they've been a small child, to the point where people no longer give it much thought.

Disney is a very big term that can cross over to many different forms of media such as movies, books, comics, television shows, social media, and so many more things that can be considered a normal part of everyday life to a large vast number of people. Disney has also managed to make its way beyond any movie as it's implemented itself into regular stores and grocery stores giving them opportunities to reach audiences at any point and time of the day.

"Damsels in Discourse: Girls Consuming and Producing Identity Texts Through Disney Princess Play" by Karen E. Wohlwend (2009), researches how children enact what they have seen and heard through their exposure to Disney in their real life. Wohlwend goes into depth about how little girls become big consumers of the Disney princess line and how their views on what they see the Disney Princesses do, wear, act, all. Influence their values, perspective, personality, etc. A book that has a ton of research And to name another research article that pertains to it, "Understanding Disney" (2001) published by Janet Wasko, takes the company as a whole under investigation and discusses their potential influence and power in society. Even though the book was written nineteen years ago, it still manages to stay relevant due to the fact that what is discussed in the book is still relevant to how Disney acts and performs with their business today. The influence Disney media has on its audience is of the utmost importance as it can affect how people communicate and behave towards other people, because children are very malleable to the content they absorb in their younger years.

It's important to remember that Disney is and always has remained a business despite its smaller upbringing back in 1923. The aim and goal of the company seem to be to expand its universe and bring in as much money for stockholders as possible (Wasko, 2001a). They operate in two ways: The Disney/ABC Television Group and ESPN Inc.[49] Disney's holdings also include studio entertainment like Broadway shows, albums, consumer products, Internet and direct marketing, and various media networks (Wasko, 2001b). Not only that, but Disney has six theme parks that are accompanied by gigantic and extravagant resorts with hotels and vacation opportunities. It's come to a point where Walt Disney World Resort in the United States is not just popular among tourists but is a hot spot for corporate tourism as well (Wasko, 2001a). Even if theme parks might seem out of their area of expertise, it still represents one of their main goals. Disney has managed to branch out its theme parks to many different places such as California, Florida, and international locations such as Tokyo, Paris, Hong Kong, and Shanghai.[50] Disney has slowly been opening up more locations over the years and with cruise lines as well, Disney domination doesn't stop in those specific locations.

Marketing is the name of Disney's game and their goal is to always be the talk of the town and to keep people pulled in and interested. Disney achieves this through a wide network while not damaging its aim to promote family values. To assist in this Disney is not shy about their product marketing of books, novels, comics, and just branding in general. For example, when I walked into my hometown Target when *Frozen 2* had just recently come out, the first thing I saw was a rack dedicated fully to their merchandise. Having their business reach

---

[49] http://thewaltdisneycompany.com/disney-companies
[50] https://dpep.disney.com/

across so many different areas can give them dominance throughout media and stores everywhere. Disney is well crafted and trained in creating events to promote its material, as well as promoting an upcoming movie at children's festivals that don't have any connection to products of theirs. (Wasko, 2001a). Disney will often promote themselves in secret ways through product placement in television shows, or getting a person to buy merchandise to walk around with and advertise that for themselves. It's also no secret that because of the wide variety of Disney products and marketing across the world, even if Disney were to stop making movies, they would still have a gigantic amount of money coming in from their other resources.

I interviewed the biggest Disney fan I know, Izabella Bishop, who is a twenty-year-old female who happened to grow up majorly influenced by Disney. I had chosen to discuss this topic with her because I knew this isn't something she would normally think about but has been influenced by Disney's marketing throughout her life. While movies are the ideas people cling onto the most when it comes to Disney, I asked her a variety of questions about many other aspects of Disney as well. Izabella was not shy about stating her love for the franchise and company to her friends and family, which is a question I think could change depending on the type of person you are whether it be gender, age, etc. I also tried to find out her connection with Disney through the media and online. She responded by talking about how she is connected through Disney on multiple social media platforms such as Instagram, Facebook, and even Snapchat. This is through connecting to specific movies, the company itself, and Disney World. When I had brought up to the interviewee what her relationship with Disney was offline, at first, she was adamant that her only real connection with Disney offline is through movies and tv shows that she would watch regularly, especially with the new Disney Plus streaming website that had just recently come out. However, after I had brought up the points of marketing and products she owned, she realized that she was coming in contact every day through clothing, towels, school supplies for college, collectibles in her room, her phone case, etc. I then had asked her why she believes she would own all of this merchandise and the connections behind it. She discussed how Disney has a ton of memories through her family, adoration of its characters, and growing up with it as a child because there was a whole channel dedicated to it as well on cable. "Disney has always been a huge part of my life just because of how it was a form of entertainment that I grew up with and my family adored. I was a Hannah Montana fan girl, loved every Disney channel animated movie, and was a sucker for any Minnie and mickey mouse merchandise. It was always something the whole family could watch together, never get tired of, and would quote constantly. Mulan the movie is an example as we'd jokingly quote it to each other." My final question was if any influence she believed Disney had on her and any influence that was detected to her was positive throughout the whole media as in your typical life lessons, happy ending, etc.

This research was aimed at looking at research that was previously done on Disney, the influence the company had on people, opening up perceptions about the corporate brand. An overview of the media shows how much people are connected to Disney through their everyday life so often that they will not even notice it. But what was most significant through this research is how the audience is becoming or has already been the interest to companies and creators alike, as they're beginning to become walking billboards with free advertisement as they freely promote products they are fond of. Overall the results showed that the presence of Disney can be huge and magnificent within someone's life nowadays to the point where no matter where someone could be looking, they just might be looking at something Disney had their hands on to continue to dominate and grow even bigger.

Recently many cellular services around the world have started implementing 5G towers. 5G promises mobile data speeds that far outstrip the fastest home broadband network currently available to consumers. Many civilians have voiced their opinions on the risk that 5G towers may have on their health. 5G represents the fifth generation of wireless communications technologies supporting cellular data networks. Large-scale adoption began in 2019 and today virtually every telecommunication service provider in the developed world is upgrading its infrastructure to offer 5G functionality. Though this idea may seem very logical and will be an improvement to communication, the concerns that many have about it, is the radiation that it produces. While other countries have already started testing the variety of significant features it uses, An article The New York Times published May 12th, of 2019 states "It targets a new world of interconnected, futuristic technologies that would reach into consumers' homes, aid national security and spark innovative industries. Already, medical firms are linking up devices wirelessly to create new kinds of health treatments." [51] Because 5G towers provide us with a faster and more reliable connection, does the risk that it may potentially have on human health outweigh the reward?

The advantages of 5G network and its innovations would not only provide higher cellular speeds but 5G could even usher in a new era of "smart cities" in which energy grids, traffic signals, and emergency services are linked to reduce inefficiencies.[52] The technology of 5G potentially would be groundbreaking as it could provide the extra bandwidth to create a network capable of linking cars and robots, in

---

[51] Broad, William j. "Your 5G Phone Wont Hurt You. But Russia Wants You to Think Otherwise." *The New York Times*, May 12, 19AD b.
[52] Campanaro, Amanda. "What Is 5G? The next Wireless Revolution Explained," March 12, 18AD.

addition to phones and computers. Some common questions many consumers have are:

> ➤ "Will I need a new phone?",
> ➤ "When will 5G be available", and
> ➤ "What are the advantages of 5G?"

Unfortunately as we saw with previous generation upgrades, new phones would be a requirement in order to use 5G network. Companies such as Samsung have already released phones that are compatible with 5G networks. As this phone was released, they used the slogan stating "Stay ahead of tomorrow." The spread of 5G tower is quite mainstream, as of now 40 countries have started building infrastructures. The United States is currently still in the testing phase of 5G technology. Many cellular companies are capitalizing on this opportunity to test 5G as towers are constructed in larger cities. Sprints 5G services are now available in Atlanta, Dallas, Houstons, Chicago, Phoenix, and Washington D.C.

With 4.6 billion people using cell phones daily the concerns many have expressed about the risk of 5G   radiation is reasonable. With radiation frequency so high, it poses a major health concern of the people living in a thousand mile radius of one of these towers. The information given to the public is very slim and can be confusing if not explain correctly. Dr. Steve Novella, an assistant professor of neurology at Yale, iterates . "Using the term radiation is misleading because people think of nuclear weapons—they think of ionizing radiation that absolutely can cause damage. It can kill cells. It can cause DNA mutations." But since non-ionizing radiation doesn't cause DNA damage or tissue damage, Novella says that most concern about cell phone RFR is misplaced. "There's no known mechanism for most forms of non-ionizing radiation to even have a biological effect.[53] Research regarding the potential risk

---

[53] Johnson, Dave. "How Worried Should You Be About the Health Risks of 5G?" How. How-To Geek, March 31, 2020.

of 5G seems very minimum due to the fact that 5G is fairly new and radiation research is often inconclusive and can take a long time for real results to show.

One may also question "How economical is 5G technology?" The social impact on 5G could have an immediate effect on society. With the advancement of 5G networking can be practical as it will be contributing to, enhancing infrastructure, while promoting sustainable industrialization and promoting new ideas. The spread of 5G networks may come as a economical burden at first as it would take $20,000 to build one tower. GMSA, an industry organisation that represents the interests of mobile network operators worldwide, predicts 5G will provide a $2.2 trillion global economy of the next 15 years.

With so little knowledge researchers have on 5G network is it reliable enough to ensure it won't cause significant health risk to humans in the future? We've seen many examples throughout history where innovations have looked efficient and pose no health risk until years later, where the damage becomes irreplaceable. For example, the most concerning issue affecting the entire population is climate change. For over 200 years humans have been producing greenhouse gasses into the atmosphere with little to any knowledge of what could affect the health of the environment in the future now the damage that has been inflicted on the environment for instance the glaciers that are melting at an alarming rate in Antarctica. Without the advancement of 5G technology it would possibly mean the U.S. would lack the latest technology needed to stay ahead of our competition, but with it could pose a threat to human health.

Mariah Dobson

The COVID-19 epidemic is an event that has changed the way people do things around the world. It will be a subject in the history books for the next generation to be quizzed on, but how much do we know about the Coronavirus that is rampaging the world? Thankfully there is a lot of information for those who wish to find more by simply searching the internet.

COVID-19 is an acronym from the World Health Organization that stands for coronavirus disease of 2019[54] but it has been called many other things like Corona Virus, Corona, Rona, Chinese Virus, and the Wuhan Disease. Though many aren't official or even ethical most people have heard COVID-19 called one of these names in the time of the epidemic. It's important to note the different names because depending on what you type in your search bar you will get different kinds of articles. Some may be educational, from scientific organizations, or some may be from the public, some of which don't have very much or correct information.

Typing "COVID-19" into the google search bar brings you alerts, a section on the left with an overview, symptoms, preventions, treatments, news, and statistics, top stories including "Exclusive: 'Idon't think anybody was ready for this Covid' says head of federal prisons" by CNN, "Animal Viruses Are Jumping to Humans. Forest Loss Makes IT Easier." by The New York Times, and "You Can Get COVID- Friendly Vegan Chocolate Easter Bunnies" byLiveKindly. Following top news stories are sections for help and information, safety tips, symptoms, and a map of affected areas, then other articles.

---

[54] Vergnaud, Sophie. "What Does COVID-19 Stand For in Its Full Form and Who Named It?" The GoodRx Prescription Savings Blog, April 10, 2020. https://www.goodrx.com/blog/what-does-covid-19-mean-who-named-it/.

Searching "Coronavirus" brings many of the same results. The info in the left, top news stories "Coronavirus Live Updates : U.S, Surpasses Italy in Total Number of Confirmed Deaths" by The New York Times, "Live Updates: U.S. surpasses Italy for most confirmed deaths with more than 20,000" by Washington Post, and "Jane Goodall blames 'disregard for nature' for coronavirus pandemic" by The Hill. Following these articles are sections for help and information local and national resources, and local and health authorities on twitter, then more articles and top results relating to coronavirus.

If you search "Corona", Google will show you the same section on the left, top stories including "How long does the corona virus live on different surfaces?" by The Guardian, "Coronavirus updates:More than half a million people have tested positive in the U.S." by CBS News, and "Coronavirus live updates: $1,000 fines for shelter-in-place violations in Santa Cruz" by San Francisco Chronicle. Following this is are sections of help and information, local and national resources, and then articles relating to corona.

Google searching "Rona" doesn't bring many articles or information relating to Covid-19. The Top stories are "'Rona needs to stay away. Too many people need me." by Washington Post, and "7 slang words Gen Zers coined in the coronavirus era, and what they actually mean" by Business Insider. After that there are articles for stores and renovation tips.

Searching "Chinese Virus" brings up the same section in the left as searching Covid-19 and Corona, then top news stories including "Bill Maher blasts 'PC' uproar over 'Chinese virus' label: 'we SHOULD blame China'" by Fox News, Bill Maher Says Coronavirus Should Be Called the 'Chinese Virus': 'We Should Blame China'" by The Wrap, and Bill Maher Defends Calling Coronavirus the 'Chinese Virus'" by Variety. After the top stories are sections for common questions, prevention, and other articles of other people, including President Trump, defending calling Coronavirus 'The Chinese Virus'.

If you search "Wuhan Disease" you aren't met with many of the news or information sections but with wikipedia pages and articles saying that it should be called the Wuhan virus and talking about "The Bat Woman" in Wuhan China.

The more controversial names didn't have the public health information like the CDC recognized titles. It is important to think about what the title and the source of the information you're looking at are. Many authors use titles to grab their attention and usually have surface-level knowledge. If you want good information, check to see if the article is written by an educational source or if the title seems attention-grabbing or informative[55].

What you type into your search bar matters. Using a keyword works great when you are lightly researching something but if you want to get a rounded idea of your topic, I recommend using many different keywords. You will get more articles with a variety of information on your topic.

---

[55] Alyssa Luukkonen - Email Interview April 22, 2020

On the website IMDb, or Internet Movie Database, there exists a page titled the "Top Rated TV Shows." This list, as rated by IMDb users, gives a full list of the 250 highest rated TV shows on the website. As of April 15, 2020, the two highest rated shows on the website are *Planet Earth II* and *Planet Earth*, with a rating of 9.5 and 9.4, respectively.[56] Following that, there are at least fifteen more documentaries on the list. Documentaries are nothing new, having been around for nearly a century, but recently documentaries have become more a household thing, with shows like *Making A Murderer* and *Tiger King* taking the nation by storm. Which begs the question: Why do people enjoy documentaries?

In 2004, a man named Michael Moore released a movie called *Fahrenheit 9/11*, which made $119 million dollars and became the highest grossing documentary film of all time.[57] In 2015, Netflix released *Making A Murderer*, which after only 35 days on the site had reached a total of 19.3 million viewers.[58] Now, in 2020, Netflix released *Tiger King*, which reached 34 million viewers in its first 10 days.[59] Clearly, people's love of documentaries has been around for a while, even before the days of streaming services.

"I used to go see these movies all the time,"[60] said Rob Larson, a communications professor at the College of St. Scholastica, when asked

---

[56] "IMDb Top Rated TV Shows." IMDb. IMDb.com. Accessed April 15, 2020.

[57] Gleiberman, Owen. "How Michael Moore Lost His Audience." Variety. Variety, September 24, 2018.

[58] Nededog, Jethro. "Here's How Popular Netflix's 'Making a Murderer' Really Was According to a Research Company." Business Insider. Business Insider, February 12, 2016.

[59] Spangler, Todd. "'Tiger King' Nabbed Over 34 Million U.S. Viewers in First 10 Days, Nielsen Says (EXCLUSIVE)." Variety. Variety, April 8, 2020.

[60] Larson, Rob. Interview by Jack Hagberg. Personal Interview. Minnesota, April 12, 2020.

about how the viewing of documentaries has changed over time. "I think the success {of Tiger King} comes from an entertaining documentary mixed with the current situation." When asked why he thinks that people enjoy documentaries, Rob responded by saying, "I think because we have a long tradition of storytelling... we're hungry for information... for learning about being in the world; what it's like for others to exist." When asked why he personally enjoys documentaries, Rob said, "I like the entertainment value and the informational value."

But Rob is not the only one who feels this way. In his book, *Introduction to Documentary*, American film critic Bill Nichols writes, "The golden age of documentaries began in the 1980s. It continues unabated.... These films challenge assumptions and alter perceptions. They see the world anew and do so inventively."[61] This is the basis for people's love of documentaries. They introduce people to a perspective that is not their own on an issue that they otherwise might not have learned about. David Attenborough[62] is one such name that comes to mind. Throughout all of his work on series such as *Planet Earth I & II*, *Blue Planet I & II*, and *Frozen Planet*, all of which appear on the top 250 IMDb movies list, he has tried to inform and educate his audience about how astonishing the world outside their own homes is. Many of these shows take place in places that almost the entirety of the audience does not have access to, such as the Amazon Rainforest and the depths of the Arctic Ocean. By doing this, he informs his audience about things that most people learn in high school science, but does so in an arguably more entertaining way (depending on the science teacher). As entertaining as the David Attenborough documentaries are however, not everyone enjoys learning about nature. Some people would rather learn about material that may be considered darker.

One of the most popular types of documentary is true crime documentaries. These are documentaries that explore and examine

---

[61] Nichols, Bill. *Introduction to Documentary.* Bloomington, IN: Indiana University Press, 2017.
[62] "David Attenborough." *IMDb*, IMDb.com

real-life crimes. This includes series like *The Jinx*, *Making A Murderer*, and *Tiger King*. While these documentaries are highly informational, they're also striving to entertain their audience, so that the audience gets hooked on the show. Many true crime series play out like fictional TV shows, with cliffhangers and twists becoming a large part of the show. A large part of the appeal comes from the knowledge that these stories are true, no matter how fictionalized they may seem, and that the people in these stories are in many ways similar to the viewer (apart from, of course, the enacting of the crime). "Over thousands and thousands of years we've fine tuned in our brains this desire to hear accounts of others and even of our own lives relating to one another."[63] When looking at the elements that make up and contribute to true crime stories, it is easy to see why so many people enjoy viewing them.

Not all true crime series deal with murder. Some series, such as *McMillions*, take a subject that is less gruesome. It gives the details on the scam that allowed people to cheat millions out of the McDonald's Monopoly game in the 1990s. While the theft of millions of dollars is no laughing matter, the series takes a more comical and lighthearted approach in its delivery, especially thanks to its unique and eccentric cast. Series like these appeal to all types, but are much more accessible to those that may not enjoy hearing about how a famous businessman cut up a body and threw it in a bay. Another example of a more lighthearted documentary is *Fyre*, which looks at the "creation" of the would-be FYRE music festival. These documentaries are conducted in the same style as those that contain more gruesome material, and play out in the same way, but are much more welcoming for those that may be faint of heart.

But crime and nature are far from the only types of documentaries. Many famous directors, such as Jim Jarmusch[64] and Peter

---

[63] Larson, Rob. Interview by Jack Hagberg. Personal Interview. Minnesota, April 12, 2020.

[64] "Gimme Danger." IMDb. IMDb.com, August 5, 2016.

Bogdanovich[65], have tried their hand at a music documentary. A show like *How It's Made* deals with the creation of everything and anything. *Cops* is another popular documentary series, although many people do not realize that it is considered a documentary series, as it appears to be almost fictional. There are hundreds if not thousands of documentary films/series to choose from, which is the reason that people enjoy them so much.

From nature to crime to music and many more, there's a documentary for everyone. This is why so many people enjoy the genre. There is something out there for everyone, no matter what their interests may be. For those that like more scientific material, there are series like *Planet Earth*. For those that enjoy true crime shows, there are series like *The Jinx*. Once one dives into the rabbit hole that is the viewing of documentaries, it is easy to get hooked on series after series. That is why people love documentaries.

---

[65] "Tom Petty and the Heartbreakers: Runnin' Down a Dream." IMDb. IMDb.com, October 14, 2007.

In 2019, Marvel fans were dismayed to hear that one of their favorite superheros, Tom Holland's Peter Parker/Spiderman, would be leaving the Marvel Cinematic Universe (MCU) due to contract disputes between Disney, who owns Marvel Studios, and Sony, who owns the rights to the character of Spiderman. This news came as a surprise to many; when we consume media, oftentimes we don't give much thought to where it comes from. Fortunately, the two companies were eventually able to come to an agreement, and Spiderman will return to the MCU for at least two more films. This negotiation was a recent and quite public example of how media ownership can affect the content of media that is produced. However, the discussion surrounding media ownership, specifically the concentration of media ownership, runs far deeper than superheros.

Just exactly how concentrated is the media? Linda Holtzman and Leon Sharpre[66] state that the concentration of media ownership has increased in the last fifty years; "By 2008, the 'U.S. media landscape' was 'dominated by massive corporations that, through a history of mergers and acquisitions, have concentrated their control over what we see, hear and read. In many cases, these giant companies are vertically integrated, controlling everything from initial production to final distribution'" (41). According to Kelly Mullan, a communications faculty at The College of Saint Scholastica, there are only eight corporations that own most of what we see on television: Fox, Disney, Viacom, Comcast, AT&T, Discovery, Cable Vision, and Scripps. To further demonstrate, let's take a closer look at one of these media giants and its assets.

---

[66] From the book *Media Messages: What Film, Television, and Popular Music Teach Us About Race, Class, Gender, and Sexual Orientation*

The article "Your Complete Guide to Everything Owned by Comcast" on Nasdaq.com details all of the companies that are under the ownership of Comcast. Comcast owns: Universal Studios (as well as the Universal Studios Parks and Resorts), DreamWorks Animation, NBC Universal (which includes television channels like NBC, CNBC, MSNBC, USA Network, Bravo, E!, and SyFy, to name a few), The Weather Channel Companies, Universal Networks International, part of Hulu, and cable companies like Group W Cable, AT&T Broadband, Susquehanna Pfaltzgraff, Adelphia Communications Corporation, and Xfinity. This list is not exhaustive but provides an idea of the breadth of Comcast's ownership.

Surrounding this concentrated media scene is a significant debate as to whether or not media ownership should be regulated. Let's begin with the argument for regulation. The more concentrated the media ownership, or the less owners, the fewer voices, perspectives, and ideas are presented to the public. Both Holtzman and Sharpe, as well as the article "Metrics, models, and the meaning of media ownership" by Des Freedman, discuss scholar Ben Bagdikian's thoughts on media ownership. "The power to 'treat some subjects briefly and obscurely but others repetitively and in depth' is where the power of concentrated ownership is most apparent. And as in social cognitive theory, 'continuous repetition and emphasis create high priorities in the public mind and in government' (Bagdikian 1997, 16)" (Holtzman & Sharpe 41). For example, a media owner may shy away from subjects they deem controversial or different in favor of more tried-and-true "family friendly" content to attract advertisers. As a result, media consumers are presented with the same ideas over and over again and miss out on other perspectives. The regulation of media ownership could allow for the inclusion of more owners and more viewpoints.

Freedman also addresses the counter-argument, providing the reasons why some feel media ownership should not be regulated. "The most common argument is technological: that in a brave new world of digital developments and consumer choice, there is little need to worry about oligopoly or a lack of diversity. The dizzying speed of technological innovation and market adaptation make redundant most attempts to control artificially the structure of markets or the preferences of consumers" (Freedman 177). In other words, due to the development of the internet, we now have access to more information than we've ever had before, so it isn't necessary to regulate existing media companies. Other arguments state that media regulation puts media businesses at a "disadvantage" when they need to be able to compete in the "new digital environment," would "constrain the innate creativity unleashed by market forces," and conflicts with the First Amendment's freedom of expression (Freedman 178-9).

However, the existence of the internet doesn't necessarily eliminate the concerns of media ownership concentration. In fact, the internet itself can be concentrated. Rodney Benson, a professor at New York University[67], said "In the US, today, market concentration is especially a concern relative to digital platforms like Google and Facebook, which are hoarding almost all of the online advertising revenues; their near monopoly has also given them free rein to use their algorithms (especially at Facebook) to highlight sensational and polarizing messages and images that keep people on their platforms as long as possible" (72). Following this logic, not only does the internet *not* refute the need for media ownership regulation, but might actually require it.

The idea of regulating media ownership is not a recent phenomenon, nor is it exclusive to the United States. "Some of the founding scholars of communications and cultural studies identified diversified ownership as central to the ability of media to pursue an independent, imaginative and critical role in public life" (Freedman 171). Freedman also mentions there are debates in places like Mexico, the United Kingdom, and Australia over stricter media ownership regulation.

---

[67] From the interview "How Media Ownership Matters in the US: Beyond the Concentration Debate."

Benson argues that it's not just a matter of the level of media ownership concentration, but more of the form of ownership that's the problem. He identifies several forms of media: stock market traded, private, state-owned, and civil society. Benson states that the most concentrated forms of ownership in the U.S. are stock market traded and private, who are "hypercommercial" and "put profits above public service" (81). In the end, he sees the diversity of forms of media as essential. "In sum, the problem is not just raw concentration of media outlets, but the concentration of forms of ownership where one form of ownership tends to dominate over all others" (83).

Bibliography

"3 Stats That Show What Memes Mean to Gen Z & Millennials." YPulse, March 5, 2019.
https://www.ypulse.com/article/2019/03/05/3-stats-that-show-what-memes-mean-to-gen-z-millennials/.

Baihley Marie, WDIO News Journalist Interview.

Benson, Rodney. 2019. "How Media Ownership Matters in the US: Beyond the Concentration Debate." *Societes Contemporaines*, no. 113 (January): 71–83. http://search.ebscohost.com.akin.css.edu/login.aspx?direct=true&db=sih&AN=138528103&site=ehost-live&scope=site.

Broad, William j. "Your 5G Phone Wont Hurt You. But Russia Wants You to Think Otherwise. The New York Times, May 12, 19AD.

Brockmyer, Jeanne F. "Media Violence, Desensitization, and Psychological Engagement." In *The Oxford Handbook of Media Psychology*, 212–20. Oxford University Press, 2014.

Campanaro, Amanda. "What Is 5G? The next Wireless Revolution Explained," March 12, 2018_.https://www.nbcnews.com/mach/tech/what-5g-next-wireless-revolution-explained-ncna855816

College of St. Scholastica, Dr. Nathan Carroll Interview

"David Attenborough." *IMDb*, IMDb.com www.imdb.com/name/nm0041003/?ref_=nv_sr_srsg_0.

"Defining the Surveillance State." Privacy International. Accessed April 15, 2020. https://privacyinternational.org/blog/1513/defining-surveillance-state.

"Disney - Leadership, History, Corporate Social Responsibility." The Walt Disney Company. Accessed April 22, 2020. http://thewaltdisneycompany.com/disney-companies.

"Disney Parks, Experiences and Products." Disney Parks, Experiences and Products, April 13, 2020. https://dpep.disney.com/.

Eberhart, George M. "Media Literacy in an Age of Fake News." American Libraries, 2019, 38–41.

Effron, Daniel A., and Medha Raj. "Misinformation and Morality: Encountering Fake-News Headlines Makes Them Seem Less Unethical to Publish and Share." Psychological Science (0956-7976) 31, no. 1 (January 2020): 75–87. http://search.ebscohost.com.akin.css.edu/login.aspx?direct=true&db=s3h&AN=141232253&site=eds-live&scope=site.

Evanson, Cara, and James Sponsel. "From Syndication to Misinformation: How Undergraduate Students Engage with and Evaluate Digital News." Communications in Information Literacy 13, no. 2 (September 2019): 228–50. doi:10.15760/comminfolit.2019.13.2.6.

Freedman, Des. 2014. "Metrics, Models and the Meaning of Media Ownership."
    International Journal of Cultural Policy 20 (2): 170–85.
    doi:10.1080/10286632.2012.752821.

Freeze, Melanie, Mary Baumgartner, Peter Bruno, Jacob R. Gunderson, Joshua Olin,
    Morgan Quinn Ross, and Justine Szafran. "Fake Claims of Fake News: Political
    Misinformation, Warnings, and the Tainted Truth Effect." *Political Behavior*,
    May 2020. https://doi.org/10.1007/s11109-020-09597-3.

Gass, Robert H, and John S Seiter. *Persuasion: Social Influence and Compliance
    Gaining.* S.l.: CRC PRESS, 2019.

"Gimme Danger." IMDb. IMDb.com, August 5, 2016
    https://www.imdb.com/title/tt1714917/?ref_=nv_sr_srsg_0.

Gleiberman, Owen. "How Michael Moore Lost His Audience." Variety. Variety,
    September 24, 2018.
    https://variety.com/2018/film/columns/how-michael-moore-lost-his-audience-
    fahrenheit-11-9-1202953813/.

Griffin, Andrew. "Government Shares Scams and False Stories Trying to Benefit from
    Coronavirus Outbreak." The Independent. Independent Digital News and
    Media, March 30, 2020.
    https://www.independent.co.uk/life-style/gadgets-and-tech/news/coronaviru
    s-government-scam-misinformation-rumours-hoax-message-whatsapp-covid
    -19-a9436316.html.

"Intelligence Brief: How Much Will We Pay for 5G?" Mobile World Live, June 13, 2019.
    https://www.mobileworldlive.com/blog/intelligence-brief-how-much-will-we-p
    ay-for-5g/.

Holtzman, Linda, Leon Sharpe, and Joseph Farand Gardner. *Media Messages: What
    Film, Television, and Popular Music Teach Us About Race, Class, Gender, and
    Sexual Orientation.* 2nd ed. Armonk, New York: M.E.Sharpe, 2014.

"IMDb Top Rated TV Shows." IMDb. IMDb.com.
    https://www.imdb.com/chart/toptv?ref_=tt_awd.

Jeffrey, Carys. Interview by Emily Wabik. Personal Interview, April 14, 2020.

Johnson, Dave. "How Worried Should You Be About the Health Risks of 5G?"
    How-To Geek, March   31, 2020.
    https://www.howtogeek.com/423720/how-worried-should-you-be-about-the-h
    ealth-risks-of-5g/..

Johnson, Ashley. Interview by Emily Wabik. Personal Interview, April 13, 2020.

Kim, Madeline. "Evolving Memes Influence Society in Unexpected Ways." The Tartan,
    October 8, 2017. https://thetartan.org/2017/10/9/forum/meme.

Lankov, Andrei Nikolaevich, In-ok Kwak, and Choong-Bin Cho. "The Organizational Life:
    Daily Surveillance and Daily Resistance in North Korea." *Journal of East Asian
    Studies* 12, no. 2 (2012): 193–214. doi:10.1017/S1598240800007839.

Larson, Rob. Interview by Jack Hagberg. Personal Interview. Minnesota, April 12, 2020.

Mian, Areeb, and Shujhat Khan. "Coronavirus: the Spread of Misinformation." *BMC / Medicine* 18, no. 1 (March 18, 2020): 1–2. https://doi.org/10.1186/s12916-020-01556-3.

Mistry, Eric. Interview by Jacob Stiele. Personal Interview, March 30, 2020.

Moravec, Patricia, Randall Minas, and Alan R. Dennis. "Fake News on Social Media: People Believe What They Want to Believe When It Makes No Sense at All." *SSRN Electronic Journal*, 2018. https://doi.org/10.2139/ssrn.3269541.

Mullan, Kelly. Personal interview, 13 April 2020.

Nededog, Jethro. "Here's How Popular Netflix's 'Making a Murderer' Really Was According to a Research Company." Business Insider. Business Insider, February 12, 2016. https://www.businessinsider.com/netflix-making-a-murderer-ratings-2016-2.

Nesvig, Ben. Interview by Emily Manning. Personal Interview, April 10, 2020.

Newman, Nic. "Journalism, Media, and Technology Trends and Predictions 2020." *Digital News Project*, January 2020, 1–40.

Newton, Casey. "Google Uses Location Data to Show Which Places Are Complying with Stay-at-Home Orders - and Which Aren't." The Verge. The Verge, April 3, 2020. https://www.theverge.com/2020/4/3/21206318/google-location-data-mobility-reports-covid-19-privacy.

Nichols, Bill. "The Voice of Documentary." *Film Quarterly* 36, no. 3 (1983): 17–30. https://fq.ucpress.edu/content/ucpfq/36/3/17.full.pdf

Nichols, Bill. *Introduction to Documentary*. Bloomington, IN: Indiana University Press, 2017.

Pennycook, Gordon, Jonathon Mcphetres, Yunhao Zhang, and David Gertler Rand. "Fighting COVID-19 Misinformation on Social Media: Experimental Evidence for a Scalable Accuracy Nudge Intervention," 2020. https://doi.org/10.31234/osf.io/uhbk9

Pennycook, Gordon, and David G. Rand. "Fighting Misinformation on Social Media Using Crowdsourced Judgments of News Source Quality." *Proceedings of the National Academy of Sciences* 116, no. 7 (February 12, 2019): 2521–26. https://doi.org/10.1073/pnas.1806781116.

Qiang, Xiao. "The Road to Digital Unfreedom: President Xi's Surveillance State." *Journal of Democracy* 30, no. 1 (2019): 53-67. doi:10.1353/jod.2019.0004.

Rosenthal, Alan, and John Corner. *New Challenges for Documentary*. Manchester: Manchester University Press, 2012.

Scott, Veronica, and Timothy Bill. 2018. "Memes: The Interaction Between Imagery and Subculture An Analysis of Situation, Race, and Gender on the Pi Kappa Delta Social Media App." *Forensic* 103 (1): 33–51.

Siegel, Jacob. "Is America Prepared for Meme Warfare?" Vice, January 31, 2017. https://www.vice.com/en_us/article/xyvwdk/meme-warfare.

Spangler, Todd. "'Tiger King' Nabbed Over 34 Million U.S. Viewers in First 10 Days,
        Nielsen Says (EXCLUSIVE)." Variety. Variety, April 8, 2020.
        https://variety.com/2020/digital/news/tiger-king-nielsen-viewership-data-str
        anger-things-1234573602/.

Sullivan, Katie. "The Fox 'News' Lie: Fox's 'News' Side Pushed Misinformation Every Day
        for Four Months Straight." Media Matters for America. Accessed April 16, 2020.
        https://www.mediamatters.org/fox-news/fox-news-lie.

The Jinx: The Life And Deaths Of Robert Durst. Directed by Andrew Jarecki. Written by
        Andrew Jarecki, Marc Smerling, Zachary Stuart-Pontier. HBO, 2015.

"Tom Petty and the Heartbreakers: Runnin' Down a Dream." IMDb. IMDb.com, October
        14, 2007. https://www.imdb.com/title/tt0965382/?ref_=rvi_tt.

Wardle, Claire. "A New World Disorder." Scientific American 321, no. 3 (September 2019):
        88. http://search.ebscohost.com.akin.css.edu/login.aspx?direct=true&db=edb
        &AN=138069843&site=eds-live&scope=site.

Wasko, Janet. *Understanding Disney: the Manufacture of Fantasy.* S.l.: Polity
        Press, 2020.

Wohlwend, Karen E. "International Literacy Association Hub." International Literacy
        Association (ILA). John Wiley & Sons, Ltd, November 9, 2011. \
        https://ila.onlinelibrary.wiley.com/doi/abs/10.1598/RRQ.44.1.3.

Zacks. "Your Complete Guide to Everything Owned by Comcast." Nasdaq, n.d.
        https://www.nasdaq.com/articles/your-complete-guide-everything-owned-co
        mcast-2017-10-12.